THE UNCOMMON
MILLIONAIRE

THE UNCOMMON
MILLIONAIRE

Financial Success Begins With Behavior

ALFRED D. RIDDICK, JR.

THE UNCOMMON MILLIONAIRE

Game Time Budgeting, LLC
260 Northland Boulevard, Suite 300
Cincinnati, OH 45246
www.gametimebudgeting.com

Cover photo by Jeff Schaefer Photography
About the author photo by Easley Blessed Photography
Cover and interior design by Adina Cucicov
Edited by Bill Bagley

ISBN: 978-0-9913929-0-2
Printed in the United States of America

To my beautiful and supportive wife, Lesia.
You inspire me, love me unconditionally,
and are my best friend. Being your husband
is an honor and a pleasure.
I love you to infinity and back.

TABLE OF CONTENTS

ACKNOWLEDGEMENTS

My parents, Alfred and Alice Riddick, were the biggest influences on my life during childhood. I thank you, mom and dad, for not spoiling me with material things…but with love. Most of all, I appreciate you for instilling in me a strong work ethic. I recall a number of times you chose not to buy me hundred-dollar sneakers and name-brand shirts and jeans. You taught me how to earn my own money, buy things for myself, and understand the value of a dollar.

Thanks to my older sister, Shawanda Pauldin, for being born first. I had the privilege of learning many money and life lessons from you. I began reading the Bible and learning what "the word" says about money because of your influence. Thank you for the countless sermons on tape you mailed over twenty years ago. I believe those tapes developed my inquisitive nature. I listened intently to each of them and made an effort to implement what I learned (most of the time). As you know, I am a work in progress. I also appreciate you graduating from college and leasing the first vehicle you acquired. I will never forget your constant complaining after your Toyota Camry lease expired and you calculated its costs in lease payments and purchase price. Most people do not like being the youngest in the family, but for me it was a blessing. Your experiences provided on-the-job training.

Thank you, Sam Robinson, for providing an opportunity to wash cars and mow lawns while working at Robinson Funeral Home. Many odd jobs I completed as a child came about because of my association with you. Over the years, I learned valuable lessons about customer service and developed the foundation for my business acumen under your guidance. One of the greatest lessons you taught me was that you do not have to do something yourself if you can afford to pay someone else to do it. I think about you every time I pull into my driveway and notice my lawn has been mowed by someone else.

Chapter 1

THE CONSEQUENCES OF BEING 'UNDERINSURED'

I woke up and cooked my usual breakfast—oatmeal with honey, raisins, and a fourth of a cup of milk. Lesia, my wife, reminded me that oatmeal is "just plain nasty, I don't know how you eat that stuff." I disregard her comment as each spoonful of oatmeal satisfied my hunger. I referred to oatmeal then as I do now as my breakfast of champions. I rinse the special "oatmeal bowl" Lesia bought me for Christmas, open the dishwasher door, and place my dirty dishes inside. It's now time for work.

I walked down the 12 steps to my basement office admiring the wooden sculptures hanging on the wall while anticipating another busy workday. My normal habit was to skip the last step and jump to the bottom, feeling the soft carpet underneath my feet as I walked around the corner to my office door. This particular day, I heard a splash when my feet touched the floor. I thought, "Aw, man! I can't believe the basement flooded. This can't be happening!" I turned to the right and walked toward the couch in front of the entertainment center. Every step I took was accompanied by the sound of water being displaced. I longed for the silence associated with walking on dry carpet, but it never came.

I walked in the storage area and saw water rushing down a drainage pipe. The rapid movement of the water reminded me of Niagara Falls. My initial thought was that a pipe had burst and caused flooding in the basement. I would soon discover, in total disgust and disbelief, the true cause of the flood. I walked toward my new pool table pondering how much it cost and whether the wooden legs had survived the water damage. Luckily, there was no water near the pool table. However, the carpet in my office was saturated. There was obvious water damage to the furniture, but the electronic equipment was not harmed.

Our basement is approximately 1,500 square feet. It was finished about a year and a half before the flood. It's easy for house guests to distinguish the "girlie area" from my "man cave." One side was built to accommodate Lesia's desire for a lounging area, entertainment center, orange walls, a full bathroom, and storage space for her liturgical dance clothes. My side is painted brown with framed pictures from the civil rights era and other moments in African-American history (e.g., our feature article in *Black Enterprise*).

My initial thought was purchasing a Shop-Vac from a home improvement store to suck up the water. I went with my gut instinct, but quickly realized my efforts were in vain due to the amount of water in the basement. I felt like a hamster on a wheel—exerting a lot of energy but getting nowhere.

I called a water damage repair company and was told they could arrive within two hours. The carpet and padding were soaked. The gentlemen from the water damage company had to cut them in smaller pieces due to the extra water weight in order to carry them up the stairs. Once the damaged carpet and padding were removed, they installed four humongous dehumidifiers which would dry the sheetrock and wood. These machines operated for approximately 48 consecutive hours, while my mind focused on the amount of the next electric bill! The water damage repair guys also sprayed a chemical on the walls to prevent mold growth.

I called my insurance company to file a claim and was reminded our basement coverage was $5,000. I then realized Lesia and I had forgotten to increase the insurance coverage after finishing the basement (cost: $23,000). The pain of spending cash saved over an extended period of time made the situation worse. Spending with credit is easy; cash hurts.

The bill for removing the old carpet and padding, dehumidifying the basement, moving the pool table (twice) and installing new carpet was $7,500. This left us with a $2,500 shortfall. Lesia and I could have used that extra money for a vacation.

The basement flooded after there had been an unusual amount of rainfall. We assumed this was the cause of the flood but wondered if there was a problem with our sump pump. The purpose of a sump pump is to collect water in a basin and drive it away from the house. My wife and I decided to conduct an investigation. I removed a shelf designed to conceal the location of the sump pump. Lesia and I couldn't believe our eyes. The plug to the sump pump was not connected to the electrical outlet. We can only assume this occurred during the construction of our finished basement. Who would have thought $7,500 worth of damages could result from a three pronged cord not being plugged into an outlet?

Now is a good time to review your various insurance policies; make sure you have the proper amount of coverage. Don't just read about my financial lesson, learn from it and take action.

Chapter 2

HUMBLE BEGINNINGS

ittleton, North Carolina, where I spent my childhood, is a small town in Halifax County. It was formerly known as "little people town." The population in 2013 was 659 people (**www.city-data.com**). The first time Lesia and I traveled to Littleton, I recall her laughing uncontrollably when I said, "This is downtown." Lesia grew up in Metro Atlanta. Despite the laughter, as tears rolled down her face, she was able to ask, "Where's the rest of it?" She happily pointed out the small size of the buildings and joked that she could see from one end of downtown to the other. Littleton, the little town with the big heart, was not small to me. It was home.

The sun was shining on a cool 54 degrees autumn day as a light wind blew while my parents, Al and Alice Riddick, enjoyed a car ride through the tree-lined country roads of North Carolina. This day, November 2, 1974, would change my parents' lives as they were about to be introduced to a new bundle of joy...me. My dad drove my mom to Rocky Mount, North Carolina for the birth instead of Roanoke Rapids because he had an altercation two years before with the doctor who delivered my sister, Shawanda. This physician wanted to prescribe an epidural but my mom decided against it. After his recommendation was rejected, he rushed to the waiting room and accused my dad, mistakenly, of influencing my mom's decision. This confrontation resulted in my dad saying, "This is the last child of mine you will ever deliver." The old cliché, *say what you mean and mean what you say*, fits my dad like a glove.

I was born approximately one and a half hours after my mom and dad arrived at the hospital. Now I understand the root of my impatience; it's in my DNA. Unlike most children, I did not cry after delivery but uttered my first words..."How much will this cost?" Everyone in the delivery room was astounded to hear such clarity of thought coming from the mouth of a 10-second old baby boy.

Me as a toddler playing. Where are my clothes? Maybe mom and dad were trying to save money.

Me and my sister Shawanda

Me resting after a long day of playing

My parents did not know my gender until after I was born. Warning to expectant parents! If you name your son after his father, he'll spend at least 18 years of his life being called *junior* ... and hating it.

My dad and mom grew up in Williamston and James-ville, North Carolina, respectively. My dad, the son of sharecroppers, and my mom, reared on a family-owned farm, learned to till the soil at a young age. Al and Alice Riddick were raised in extremely modest conditions; however, my dad was the poorer of the two. His childhood home did not have running water. It did have electricity, but the family used a wood stove for heat. He shared a bedroom with his brother,

Dad's high school graduation picture   *Mom's high school graduation picture*

Ernest that could only be entered from the outside which made the cold winter nights almost unbearable. My dad's family was near the poverty level. If you've never seen an *outhouse*, I suggest you Google the word. Imagine going outside to a makeshift bathroom that consisted of a hole five feet deep in the ground surrounded by a wooden shack.

My dad had only three shirts and one pair of pants when he left Williamston for college. He used a wire to connect his soles to the rest of his shoe because they were so worn. That account may not be 100% accurate since Pops, as I call him, *has* been known to stretch the truth. Despite his modest upbringing, my dad graduated from college, obtained a master's degree, and became a teacher. His career path included becoming an elementary, middle, and high school principal. Thank God I never attended school where my dad worked. I overheard the phrase "that's Mr. Riddick's son" too many times while walking down the hallway during high school. I can't imagine what life would have been like if he and I were at the same school.

My mother's farm life consisted of manual labor, much like my dad's. Her family was not well-off; however, they owned at least 25 acres of land. During those days, late 1950s, early 1960s, that was quite an accomplishment. Mom attended Southeastern Business School after high school because she grew up always knowing what she wanted to become: an administrative assistant. When I was younger, the title was secretary. Now it's more politically correct to say administrative assistant. My mother loves to type, organize, arrange, and plan. I used to wonder why she hadn't gone to a four-year college. Now I truly admire my mother because she pursued a career doing exactly what she loves.

One of the funniest stories from my childhood involved me running around the house naked. My mom was in the kitchen baking. She must have been in a good mood that day because she hates to cook. The oven had reached her desired temperature, and she opened the door. By this time, I had become bored running naked in other parts of the house and made my way to the kitchen. The energy I exerted must have been overwhelming because I needed to sit down and catch my breath. I noticed the oven door was about the same height as my rear end so I decided to have a seat. Ouch, roasted buttocks!

There were strict rules in the Riddick household. My sister and I could only watch television for one hour after getting home from school. Once that hour was up, homework began. I dared not disobey the rules, or my older sister, Shawanda (straight A student since birth), might snitch. During my one hour of bliss, I would watch the *Transformers* and *Teenage Mutant Ninja Turtles* while enjoying my after-school snack. Now that I think about it, I don't remember having much fun after age 12. By this time, I had been introduced to the concept that work equals money. This magic formula (W=$) seemed to yield good results, so I stayed the course.

Family portrait: me, mom (Alice),
dad (Alfred Sr.), sister (Shawanda)

What does being the son of two farmers have to do with money and being debt free? First, your childhood experiences shape your view of the world. Money was not in abundant supply at the brick home my parents rented on highway 158. If I wanted more, I would have to earn it. Second, my parents instilled in me a strong work ethic. I become frustrated with people who blame others for their problems. The truth could be they are too lazy to put forth enough effort to create a better life for themselves. Finally, growing up as I did triggered one of my many early goals in life: to make more money, annually, than my dad. Parents or caretakers are the usual benchmarks for success in children's lives. I still remember the phone conversation with my dad after discovering I had finally surpassed his highest salary.

I have vivid memories of traveling to my paternal grandfather's home in Williamston to "prime" the tobacco plants. Priming is done by fieldworkers who pick the bottom leaves as they ripen. Then the bottom leaves are tied to a stick and cured with heat in a barn. The tobacco leaves are cooked until the color changes from green to the brownish color seen inside cigarettes. My job, since I was so small, was driving the tractor with the trailer attached, transporting the tobacco from the field to the barn. My dad, his brothers (Ernest, Jimmy, Tommy, and Gus), and a few family friends were responsible for plucking the leaves off the stalk one by one. I used to sit on the tractor with only one cheek touching the seat so I could press the brake.

Working in a tobacco field is not a fun job. Waking up around 5:30 in the morning to be at the field by 6:00 or 6:30 was painful. You also have to deal with the tobacco worms. Picture a fishing worm on steroids and green in color. I learned to cope with the North Carolina humidity and extremely hot temperature. Tobacco leaves are also sticky. Imagine the hottest day of your life, walking up and down rows of tobacco, plucking leaves one by one. It's hot, humid, and extremely sweat inducing. Furthermore, you're placing sticky leaves of tobacco underneath your armpit in a neatly arranged stack. My experiences in the tobacco field sparked my decision to attend college. I learned *quickly* that I preferred making money with my mind rather than by the sweat of my brow.

My payment after driving a tractor for hours in the tobacco fields of North Carolina was a carton of fruit punch and a honey bun. I didn't worry about sugar content in those days. Focusing on my treats was reason enough to endure the hot working conditions. The icing on my honey bun would melt under the intense heat which made the taste even better. It's amazing what you can get some people to do when they don't understand the value of time and money! Thanks, Dad!

Our neighbors in Littleton, Sam and Marie Robinson, were—and still are—good friends of my parents. They, along with other family members, operated Robinson Funeral Home. Growing up, they were one of only two couples I knew who ran their own business. The other couple, Mr. Willie and Carolyn Jarrell, owned a trucking company. I noticed at a young age that Sam's wife and Mr. Jarrell's wife had the nicest cars in town (a Mercedes and a Lincoln Continental). I became familiar with these cars since I washed them almost every weekend.

Sam exposed me to the life of an entrepreneur. He, like me, was focused on making money. We got along well. I was a hard worker, and Sam liked paying people who worked hard. It was a match made in heaven. He would often say, "It's hard finding people who want

Robinson Funeral Home

to work." What I heard was, "If you continue to work hard, I'll always have work for you to do." I consider Sam as my *rich* dad. He was a business owner, well-respected in the community, had a nice home, drove nice cars, and had money in the bank. I observed many people visiting the funeral home to borrow money from Sam. I realized there were only a few individuals in my world who had money... and many who did **not**. I also noticed the happy expression on Sam's face as he was lending money, in contrast to the sad look of those people *borrowing* it.

I started a lawn mowing business around age 12. The $0 startup cost was irresistible and fit my budget comfortably. My clients allowed me to use their mowers, initially. Then my dad purchased a riding mower. I had hit the big leagues. Pops should have charged a rental fee to cover the wear and tear on his equipment. But, he didn't. I also don't recall having to buy gas, either. This was a perfect deal because my only investment became *sweat equity.*

I also mowed the funeral home lawn and the lawns of family friends. I decided to expand my growing empire and started washing cars, too. I enjoyed washing cars more than mowing lawns since I couldn't—and to this day, still can't—stand the smell of freshly cut grass.

A mishap involving my dad's new riding mower provides an amusing memory from my lawn-mowing days. When I began mowing lawns we didn't have the fancy metal ramps that could be used to drive a mower onto the back of a pickup truck. Therefore, we had to depend on ingenuity. My dad drove his pickup to the end of our driveway, backed into a ditch, and I'd drive the mower onto the truck bed. One day I forgot to block the mower wheels and lock the brake before climbing into the passenger's seat. My dad pressed the accelerator and we heard the deck of the mower crash against the metal of the tailgate. I turned around just as the mower was falling to the ground. The scene was hilarious (to me), but I dared not laugh because my dad did not see the humor in it. I often thought he should have bought a bigger truck with a larger bed for hauling. We could have, at least, closed the tailgate instead of riding around with a mower hanging off the back.

Sam, the funeral home owner, permitted me to drive in funeral processions after I received my license. I was 16 and making money by wearing a suit and driving a car. *Life could not get much better.* I loved driving the hearse because the seats were comfortable, and the suspension was fantastic. It was like driving a car while sitting on your favorite couch. I could also listen to the radio, my favorite aspect of driving the hearse. (Listening to the radio while driving a family car of the deceased would have, of course, been considered rude and unprofessional.) Who was I going to disturb in the hearse?

My buddies in high school worked at fast food restaurants or other minimum-wage jobs. I support anyone who earns an honest wage, but those jobs never appealed to me. I preferred controlling my *time* and my *money*. I would start washing cars around 6:00 in the morning and be done before the temperature was too hot. I then mowed lawns toward the late afternoon as the sun was going down. Today, I hate working, lounging, or going to cookouts in the sun. Intense heat is to me like kryptonite is to Superman... not to mention the rash it causes to appear on my arms.

I developed time management and customer service skills as a young entrepreneur by creating my work schedule. I also kept a ledger itemizing the various jobs, income, and time duration. I recall averaging $15 an hour, *tax-free*. I'm grateful to everyone who allowed me to prove myself. Washing cars and mowing lawns are simple tasks. The unique trait which separated me from most others was a determination to do my best. I developed this trait when I was a youngster because I was required to re-wash the dishes until they met my parents' satisfaction. A dirty area on a car or an uncut patch of grass was unacceptable in my world of quality control. "If you're going to do something, you might as well do it right" was the consistent phrase repeated by Al and Alice Riddick.

I learned the value of assertiveness from my experiences as an entrepreneur. Many young people are afraid to ask adults to buy Girl Scout cookies, popcorn, or magazines. It's exciting when a child or teenager rings my door bell and delivers a sales pitch. There is a high probability I purchase what they're selling or make a donation to their cause. I respect them for taking the initiative and attempting to make a sale. It can be difficult overcoming your fears when attempting to sell a product to a complete stranger. Years ago, I delivered a family mandate that my nephews (Josh and Andrew) and niece (Kayla) deliver sales pitches over the phone when involved in school fundraisers. This was my way of helping them overcome shyness while learning to earn the fruit of their labor.

Parents who take their child's cookie dough or doughnut order forms to work to generate sales create a false sense of reality. This act contributes to children's lack of assertiveness. It is difficult for a child to learn the value of initiative when the opportunity to develop this trait is removed. When I operated my lawn mowing and car washing businesses, I had to make phone calls, plan my schedule, and book appointments. I learned at a young age that it is easy to make money when you do your best, please your customer, and ask for referrals.

Family trips to New Jersey were a big deal for my sister and me. One specific time, we rode in the back of my parents' new Mazda truck (the one with the too-small bed for the riding mower) from Littleton, North Carolina to East Orange, New Jersey. This trip was extra special because my parents had purchased a cab cover and made a makeshift mattress on the truck bed. You know you're 'country' when you ride for eight hours in the back of a pickup from North Carolina to New Jersey. The purpose of the trip was to visit family, but for me, it was also to use my hard-earned money to buy school clothes.

This family trip to New Jersey allowed me to purchase *Major Damage* jeans and a matching shirt. If I had purchased my clothes in Littleton or in the nearest major city, Roanoke Rapids, there is a high probability someone at my school would have had the same out-fit. I routinely paid $40 to $55 for jeans in the 90s. I don't spend that much today! I now think of dollars as something to be *invested or saved* rather than *consumed*. Had I reallocated the money spent on clothes in the past, I'm positive my net worth would now be much greater than it is. Birthdays accompanied by wisdom have allowed me to understand the value of a dollar.

I relieved some of the financial burden my parents were forced to endure by paying for my school clothes beginning at the age of 12. I wonder how many of today's teens purchase clothes or electronics with money they have earned? Parents, I observe, are determined to give their children the lives they did not have. Instead of *giving* your children the lives *you* want them to have, how about *teaching* them to *earn* the life *they* desire? There is an abundance of spoiled children, so one less of these is a step in the right direction. Although my wife and I don't have children, I've often thought parenting involved raising a responsible, independent, moral, and productive member of society.

I was accepted to North Carolina A&T State University in Greensboro during my final year of high school. I followed in my dad's footsteps and those of my sister, Shawanda. I did not realize it at the time but attending A&T had now become a family tradition. I recall my pre-teen years when my dad drove the family to the annual homecoming celebrations. My favorite events were the pre-game parade and halftime show. Watching the young female baton twirlers and flag girls entertain the crowd was especially appealing to me. I now admit, ashamedly, those events were a determining factor in my decision to attend college. Everyone needs motivation.

Since I did not secure an internship with an organization, I spent the summer following my freshman year in Littleton. I do not recall, as a freshman, attempting to obtain summer employment at a major corporation as students do today. I knew various odd jobs (i.e., mowing lawns, washing cars, driving in funeral processions) were waiting for me back home, so I was not concerned. The ability to earn money during the summer was my goal. I did not care what company or person the money came from. I had now added house painter to my list of entrepreneurial responsibilities.

Wachovia Bank and Ford Motor Company provided me with summer internships during my sophomore and junior years. One of my assignments, while with Wachovia, was conducting a feasibility study. A decision to build a bank was made as a result of some of the data I helped to collect. *Scary!* I spent the summer living in a dormitory at North Carolina State University. There is no need to document here details regarding the fun I had in a different college setting. My internship with Ford was in Houston, Texas at one of their customer service sites. My dad and I drove from Littleton to Houston… only stopping for gas, food, or to rotate driving shifts. I needed a car during the summer, so after we drove to Houston, my dad boarded a flight to Raleigh, North Carolina a few days later. The foremost memory of Houston life was my first day of work. I woke up, showered, ate breakfast, and dressed in slacks, a shirt, and tie. The walk from my apartment to my car was approximately 20 feet. I opened my apartment door and felt the Texas heat in a way I could never had imagined. It was akin to standing too close to the kerosene heater at my parent's home during the winter and feeling the sensation of the heat rapidly warming my skin. Furthermore, I hated the feeling of being over-dressed in an unusually hot environment. After I got in my car, I turned the AC to max. The heat was so intense I felt as though I would spontaneously combust. I can still see the headline—North Carolina man explodes in Texas car.

The paid summer internships supported most of my college years. However, there was one month during my senior year when I could not make ends meet. I underestimated my cost for that year. Contrary to my wishes, I decided to ask my parents for rent money. I felt lower than a pregnant ant having to ask for financial assistance. I had hit rock bottom after supporting myself since age 12. Now, at the age of 21 (adulthood),

I had to borrow money. The funny memory about this situation is how happy my parents were to provide a loan. I am guessing they were excited to lend a helping hand since I had always been so independent.

Chapter 3

YOU CAN'T MEASURE WHAT YOU DON'T TRACK

'd bet $100 that your first lesson in life involved mastering your ABC's before counting one to 100. When did it become acceptable in our society to stop counting? For example, when was the last time you counted your money? Can you recall the most recent occurrence when you purchased an item using a debit or credit card? The salesperson asked, "Will that be credit or debit?" after stating your total. When you realized the cost, there was no need to count your money, you merely swiped a card. People who lived 100 years ago could never imagine a day when someone could spend money without counting. I often hear people say, "I know I don't have much, so what's the point in counting it?" Counting your money increases awareness, develops a sense of fiscal responsibility, and helps keep score. *You can't measure what you fail to track.* Why go through the trouble of building your financial resources if you omit calculating monthly household income, expenses, and the amount saved?

I promise that your level of intimacy with money will increase dramatically when you begin to count it. This small but significant act can teach you the true value of this most important resource. If you doubt me, listen closely as I share the following. In 2013 Lesia and I spent Christmas in Atlanta with family and friends. Lesia took our niece, Kayla (whose mom had given her $20), to see *The Nutcracker*. Before taking their seats, my wife asked Kayla what she wanted from the concession stand. Kayla replied, "Nothing, I'm not hungry." This shocked Lesia because our niece, like most children her age, has little problem spending someone else's money. Ironically, since Kayla was forced to spend her *own* money, she suddenly realized the value of that twenty dollar bill… and decided to hold on to it.

Furthermore, Lesia mentioned that she and Kayla ate at a restaurant after seeing the ballet. Lesia became amused observing how our niece was deciding what to order based on how much money she'd have left after paying for her food. Kayla's exposure to fiscal responsibility reminds me of a recent quote I read by the oil tycoon J. Paul Getty, *"People who don't respect money don't have any."*

Counting your money is the initial step on the road to financial success. This process makes goal setting more realistic and provides a guide for understanding what is and is not possible. Kayla could not purchase a $30 shirt after seeing *The Nutcracker* because she had only $20. She measured her ability to afford the shirt after counting her money.

Never confuse your money with someone else's. The availability of credit has made borrowing simple and habitual. It is easy to sabotage yourself when you think of credit as money that belongs to you. Has a friend or family member recently financed a new car? Were they proud of how it shined and how it 'smelled new'? They may have driven their car to your house so you could see, touch, and smell it. You can still see the excitement on their faces and hear it in their voices while describing the features on their new car. I am often intrigued by the number of times people use the phrase *my new car* when describing that square piece of metal in the driveway sitting on four round rubber circles.

Let's explore how they have confused the rightful owners of their new car by not understanding what belongs to whom. Your friends don't *own* a new car despite the fact they signed a few sheets of paper to acquire one. They *financed* a car their lender (legal owner) is allowing them to drive *if* they make a monthly payment (which includes interest). Once people begin to understand the difference between *ownership* and *control*, then, and only then, will everyone have a more accurate assessment of how much money and wealth they have.

I challenge you to create a list detailing the value of everything you own or control (e.g., house, car, retirement accounts, and cash) versus what you owe (e.g., debt on the house, debt on the car, credit card debt, and student loans). Subtract the total of what you owe from what you own. You now have an accurate representation of your net worth or *wealth score*. This number may be negative, not as high as you thought, or higher than you thought—depending on your salary or household income.

Most people do not calculate their net worth or track spending or cash flow on a routine basis. Without accessing your online checking account, do you know the amount of your monthly pay down to the penny? If not, begin treating your personal finances like you are running a business. Every business owner needs to know how much money is coming in—and going out. These numbers are crucial to the stability and profitability of any business. The *difference* between your income and expenses... on a monthly basis... represents all the cash you have available to you in order to make your financial dreams come true.

Here's a fun exercise to help you get to know your money better.

1. Locate your checking account and credit card statements for the past two months.

2. Categorize and attach a dollar amount to your spending (e.g., housing—$1,000, transportation—$400, eating out—$300, recreation—$250, etc.)

3. Determine if there are ways to increase cash flow by A) minimizing expenses or B) increasing income.

Implement at least one *cash flow generating strategy* for the next three weeks. It may require taking your lunch to work instead of eating out; taking the bus instead of driving your car; accepting a part-time position in the evening. You will find through this exercise that there exist a number of ways to enhance cash flow. *'Hoping' for a 'financial windfall' is not one.*

Chapter 4

YOU DON'T HAVE TO BE A H.E.N.R.Y. TO ACHIEVE FINANCIAL SUCCESS

According to Avik Roy, *Forbes* opinion editor, a H.E.N.R.Y. is a *High Earner who's Not Rich Yet.* Many people incorrectly believe having more money will solve their financial distress. Some individuals, even if they inherited $1,000,000, would continue to experience money problems because their *Financial IQ* would remain 'stunted.' Have you ever looked at your paycheck or bank account statement and said to yourself, *If only I made more?* What differences in your life would there be if you did? Without a shift in mindset and modification of behaviors, everything in your financial life will remain the same. After getting laid off from a pharmaceutical sales position and losing a six-figure income, I noticed my life didn't change as dramatically as I thought it would. One of the biggest lessons I learned was how much money we were *wasting*. Before I was laid off, my wife and I frequently ate $150 dinners at local restaurants. Don't judge! That was our lifestyle at the time. Post-layoff, we adjusted our restaurant selections and discovered several dishes that taste as good, if not better, as the meals at higher-priced restaurants.

I have met many individuals whose households earn several hundred thousand dollars annually but have the same spending problems as households who earn considerably less. A high income does not mean you have the mindset required to create wealth. Some people have said there is a distinction between rich and wealthy. Tom Brady, Quarterback for the New England Patriots, is rich (net worth: $120 million). Robert Kraft (Owner of the Patriots) is wealthy (net worth: $4 billion). These sentences were written before "DeflateGate." Despite your income, whether it is low or high, you can still achieve your definition of financial success.

I remember listening to an NBA player being interviewed on a sports radio talk show many years ago. He made a troubling comment, "I might make a lot, but I also spend a lot." Truer words have never been spoken. I hope this gentleman has not added his name to the list of former professional athletes who have filed bankruptcy. A list, by the way, that is alarmingly long.

What is the meaning of *wealth* to you? I would consider myself wealthy if my wife and I had enough money to maintain our current standard of living assuming we produced zero income for the rest of our lives. Based on this definition, we *are not* wealthy. However, I believe we possess a wealth mentality. We understand the value of money and live below our means to maximize saving and investing toward our long-term goals. I know this does not sound sexy, but it is what most people do to increase their net worth, thereby increasing the probability of accumulating wealth.

Recently, I was intrigued by an article I read about wealth in America which stated that many wealthy Americans have very low levels of "earned income." Most wealthy people do not *work* for their money. They benefit from millions of dollars being generated on their behalf primarily from investments or business ventures. I wonder what it is like to be wealthy but not have an earned income! Maybe one day you and I will have this experience.

Chapter 5

CREATE *BORING* FINANCIAL SYSTEMS

have been married for almost 13 years. Lesia and I have made the same financial decisions 95% of the time. Every month, we sit in front of the computer and become broke on purpose, not by accident.

Me and Lesia

We spend every penny of the following month's income so that once it is in our possession, it already has a purpose and an assignment. When you tell your money how to behave, it follows directions. Here are some of the questions you'll hear in the Riddick household during our monthly planning sessions.

How much are we going to spend on _____?

When do you want to buy _____?

Where and when would you like to go on vacation? How much will it cost?

What would you like to do with the money left over from last month?

Christmas is coming up. What's our budget?

Who's having a birthday this month?

What concerts or plays are coming in town soon? How much are the tickets?

These questions might seem simple, *but they are effective*, which is why we've kept the same system for over a decade. You may be wondering, "Why do they stick with this program?" We like the results our system has produced in the past and we hope to repeat them in the future. Most people exhibit repetitive behaviors with money because they like the results. People who practice financial principles which produce negative results like them to a certain degree. If they did not, they would create a new system. I am sure your first thought is, *What if I don't know how to establish a new routine?* At the least, you should take the initiative to learn. Vast resources are available when individuals use four words, "Can you help me?" "Can you teach me?"

I attended a training session on whole brain thinking a few months ago. One of the most unique statements I heard the instructor, Sam Lynch, say was, "Every system is designed to get the result you're getting." This one statement had a profound impact on me. Think about your relationship with money. What systems do you implement? You may be saying, *I don't have a system.* I challenge that statement because not having a system is also a system. Have you ever heard anyone use the phrase *organized chaos*? This may be a good description of your system with money.

There are systems in my life that I like and some which require improvement. I need to resume my old system of going to the gym first thing in the morning versus waiting until evening. Morning workouts provide more energy throughout the day and allow a better night's sleep. However, I was lazy this past winter. After going to the gym in negative four degree weather, I quit and returned to my evening routine. When I go to the gym in the early morning, I get the results I am looking for. The hardest part of any journey is the first step.

Answer the following if you need help developing a financial system that works for your household:

1. Describe your current financial process after money is earned.

2. What factors or beliefs have led to your current system?

3. Determine whether you are satisfied with your results. If not, what would you like your results to be and what behaviors are you willing to modify in order to achieve these desired results?

Chapter 6

IS SAVING WORTH THE SACRIFICE?

The personal saving rate in America (the percentage of disposable income Americans set aside) is less than 6%. This implies that Americans are saving less than $6 out of every $100 of after-tax income. A saving rate this small explains why many people live the *American Nightmare* while only fantasizing about achieving the *American Dream*. Thousands of books have been and will continue to be written about how to build wealth. News flash! If you don't learn to implement discipline with money, you will always be stuck in a rut. Discipline and consistency constitute the bridge between goals and achievement. Nothing good happens until you first learn how to save money. If you don't believe the personal saving rate in America is approximately 6%, take a look at the most recent Personal Income and Outlays report from the *Bureau of Economic Analysis*.

How much of your disposable income are you saving each month? If you do not know, pay more attention to how your money is behaving. Some people choose not to base their saving rate on disposable income but on gross income instead. If this is typical in your household, my question remains the same. How much of your gross income are you saving (investments included) each month? If it is five percent, that is a start. Ten percent is better. If you are saving at least 15%, you're displaying a millionaire mindset.

Don't assume people with high annual household incomes are automatic savers or have a wealth-building mentality. These factors are mutually exclusive. The ability to save money depends more on behaviors than on how much you earn. There are more opportunities to make poor financial decisions as your income increases. How many professional athletes can you think of who have made millions during their careers only to end up filing bankruptcy? Despite the income, *save,*

save, save. For example, if a household has an annual income of $100,000 but saves $0, that's far worse than a $50,000 per year household that saves 10% (i.e., $5,000) every year. It's not how much money you earn that makes you a financial success; it's how much you *keep*. Think about all the money you've earned over your lifetime. How much do you have left?

A Georgia couple I know is dedicated to living below their means and saving for the future. They are committed to debt-free living and paid cash for two used cars within a two-year time span. Why purchase a new car when you can let someone else bear the brunt of depreciation? I spoke with this couple recently and learned they had to replace both air conditioning units in their home. In case you're wondering, they paid cash for this unexpected expense. This example serves as proof that money does what you tell it to do. What was the last command you gave your money?

I mentioned earlier that Lesia and I have a finished basement. Many people secure home equity loans for this purpose. The trend of borrowing to pay for a finished basement did not appeal to us. We decided to save and pay for the finished basement in cash. As you can imagine, finishing approximately 1,500 square feet of space wasn't cheap. However, we were willing to save the money so we wouldn't have to go into debt. Could we have applied for and received a home equity loan? Of course! We have 100% equity in our home. Why is *borrowing money* typically the number one option when people want to pay for something that is considered expensive? Receiving a loan takes the fun out of practicing *delayed gratification* until you achieve your goal. You may discover more money and wealth in your future after learning to incorporate this behavior into your daily living. Try it! You might like it.

The habit of saving must be learned if you want to achieve any type of financial goal. It doesn't matter if your objective is to save for an emergency, vacation, retirement, or braces for your child. Discipline is crucial.

Think about your current financial condition and consider where you want to be. Is saving worth the sacrifice?

Chapter 7

FORGETTING DEBT

Lesia and I were having a money discussion the other day and suddenly realized we had forgotten what it was like to have debt. I know what you are thinking. *How is that possible?* If you have been in debt for a number of years, you have grown accustomed to that aspect of your life. However, Lesia and I have grown accustomed to living *debt-free.* We became debt-free on December 21, 2007. I don't think I fully appreciate the magnitude of the impact that this might have on Lesia and me for the foreseeable future. Based on current life expectancy rates in the US, it is possible we will experience *at least 40 years of debt-free living.* I get chills just thinking about that.

I meet people on a daily basis who earn their living in the investment industry. I am a big supporter of letting your money work harder for you than you do for it. I find it interesting that I have not had one person tell me that paying off our house was a bad money move. Imagine a money manager saying, "Let's take the equity out of your house and put it in the market." If I ever come across someone who thinks like this, I'll be sure to turn around and go in the opposite direction. The true value, in my mind, of having a debt-free house is all those future mortgage payments that never have to be made. Also, peace of mind is priceless.

You can make more money in the market. I have often heard people say this when discussing whether or not to pay off a mortgage. In my opinion, that's *one huge assumption.* In the same way a market can go up, it can go down. Not one money manager can predict the future. However, I do know one thing for sure: When you do not have a mortgage, there aren't many reasons I can think of to ever borrow money again. I always say, "Maybe money can be made in the market, but it can't replace the sense of peace my wife and I have by being debt free."

Your mortgage interest deduction can save money on your taxes. I didn't and still don't believe this was ever true in our situation. Based on my calculations, we saved about $150,000 in interest by paying off our house in eight years instead of 30 years. Would I do it again? Absolutely!

When people find out my wife and I are debt free, they usually say, "Wow! How did you do that?" The answer is simple: We paid off our debt. This answer is not dramatic enough for most people because it does not contain any gimmicks, secrets, or get-rich-quick schemes. When you make the decision to pay off your debt, one of the most important things you have to do is generate as much cash flow as possible. The other important thing you have to do is stay committed to reaching your goal until it is achieved. *Discipline is key.* You have to make the gap between income and spending as wide as possible. You may have heard the old cliché that cash is king. I agree to a certain degree, but I also believe that cash flow is one of the most powerful instruments in the money game.

Let me further refute the perception that deducting mortgage interest saves money on your taxes. I'll use an excerpt from one of my educational resources, *The Financial Fitness Playbook.* Carefully review the following illustration regarding your house giving you a tax advantage.

Mortgage Amount		Interest Rate		Yearly Interest Paid
$100,000	x	5%	=	$5,000*

—Interest payment for year one only

Taxable Income		Tax Bracket		Yearly Taxes Paid
$5,000	x	25%	=	$1,250

The above example is a financial snapshot of a fictional character named John B. Free. His base salary is $48,000 a year, which puts him in the 25% tax bracket (according to 2015 tax tables). If his mortgage was paid off, he could no longer deduct the mortgage interest. In this instance, his taxable income would increase by $5,000.

Based on this example, John (like most people) is excited about giving his lender $5,000 (mortgage interest) to avoid giving the IRS $1,250 in taxes if his home was paid off. A house that's paid for means you can no longer write off mortgage interest, which means your taxable income will be higher. Re-read the previous paragraph and review the chart for clarity. Which option would you prefer?

Chapter 8

WHAT DOES HAVING MONEY REALLY MEAN?

was hanging out with my cousin, Marva, a few years ago and we started reminiscing about the old days at our maternal grandmother's home. We shared some laughs after recounting how I used to say, "When I grow up, I'm going to be a millionaire." I'm sure I didn't know what a millionaire was at the time, and I certainly didn't know any, but I guess I had it in my mind that I was going to make a million dollars a year… or at least have a million dollars someday.

In 2013, Lesia and I became what I refer to as *"faux millionaires."* This term describes millionaires whose net worth (assets minus liabilities) is equal to a million dollars, *including* the value of their primary residence. We will have become *real millionaires* by the time this book is published; that is, our net worth will exceed one million dollars, *excluding* the value of our home. Your financial IQ tends to increase as your wealth grows. When I was young, I thought a million dollars was a lot of money. Now I realize how miniscule this sum is when contemplating the amount of money required if Lesia and I decided today to stop working.

If you grew up in the South like me, there's a strong possibility you've heard people misquoting the Bible, saying, "Money is the root of all evil." The scripture they're referring to is 1 Timothy 6:10 KJV, which actually reads: For *the love* of money is the root of all evil....

How can paper currency and coins be considered evil when they do not have emotions, thoughts, or beliefs? In this physical sense, money is no different from a stick of chewing gum or a blank sheet of paper. When someone chews a stick of gum and places it under a chair or spits it out in a parking lot, is the gum evil? When representatives of PETA (People for the Ethical Treatment of Animals) pour paint over someone wearing a fur coat, is the paint evil? Money is not evil; it's the individual manipulating the money who does evil or good. The person leaving the gum behind and the person pouring paint are performing evil acts. The gum and the paint are not to blame.

Money can do much good. It builds hospitals, assists the elderly and disabled with medical care, buys canned goods for donations to less fortunate families, and supports various charities. The media glorifying lifestyles of the rich has influenced some of the value Americans place on money. Celebrity spending habits are easily determined by turning on the TV or surfing the internet. I am often intrigued by lifestyles of the young and rich who belong to the *Lucky Sperm Club* (i.e., born into privilege). I believe their lives may be a bit more challenging since most children desire to achieve more than their parents. (In fact, humans by their very nature are 10% acquisitive. In other words, no matter how much they earn or 'get,' they always want just a little bit more.) For these people, achieving a bit more may not be a possibility. If you remove financial resources from the equation, I bet their lives aren't much different from yours. Having money is a convenient resource, but, in the end, it's more important to focus on the type of person one becomes as opposed to how 'wealthy' one becomes.

Professional athletes and entertainers also play a role in this "need to be rich" mentality. Many of them own jewelry that cost more than the homes of their fans. There is nothing wrong with being able to afford anything you want when you have earned what you have (legally, of course). However, when a young person without a God-given talent for shooting three-pointers, hitting a golf ball or running as fast as humanly possible grows up thinking that is all he or she could ever do to become wealthy, that is pathetic. Why aren't student athletes with high grade point averages glorified? Heck, why aren't students with high grade point averages who aren't athletes glorified? *I believe this is where we've gotten off track as a society.*

Let's take a young man growing up in the inner city who can play basketball just as well as LeBron James, Michael Jordan, or Oscar Robertson. He might be ushered through middle school and high school because of his athletic ability, despite his scholastic ability. Keep in mind that a child athletic prodigy increases attendance at basketball games, which drives ticket sales. Many times, these individuals will get an athletic scholarship to one of the top schools in the country. College sports is a business (especially basketball and football) with inexpensive student labor cost—$0.

Now this same individual who grew up in the inner city is playing basketball for a well known university. He receives a zero cost four-year education but will likely leave college early to pursue professional sports. I wonder how that price compares to the overall increase in revenue this athlete generates for the school. There was a statistic on ESPN the other day that showed the value of the top 10 college football programs in the country. Isn't it funny that the CEO (i.e., coach) of these programs makes millions while the workers (i.e., student athletes) earn $0?

I have a personal example of the real meaning of money, which involves my paternal grandmother, Flora (R.I.P). While I was living in Vancouver, Washington, we were on the phone one day and she mentioned her bills and inability to pay them. My grandmother was not college educated nor did she finish high school. Back in those days, many children whose parents were farmers had to quit school to provide an extra pair of hands in the field.

Grandma Flora stated the amount of money she received from Social Security and from helping out during the tobacco season. It was not very much. Her job during the harvest was to string the tobacco onto a wooden stick so it could be placed in a barn for curing. During our conversation, she mentioned saving her money to pay her mortgage, taxes, and other miscellaneous items. I asked how much she owed on her house and was told a ball park figure.

After our conversation, I began to ponder how difficult making mortgage payments must be at her age, considering her declining health. Prior to this discussion, I thought my grandmother's house was paid off. I couldn't get her situation off my mind, so I decided to pay off her mortgage. I was around 22 years old at the time.

I called my parents, told them my idea, and secured their assistance with the paperwork since I lived on the west coast at the time. My dad was so moved by this gesture that he wrote a letter to me. This is significant since neither my dad nor I are letter-writing types. 18 years later, I still have it.

I had an interesting conversation about engagement rings with my wife recently. Lesia mentioned that a co-worker explained how, after the wedding, most young women end up paying for their engagement ring and wedding band. This co-worker explained that most men usually purchase the rings on a credit card. Upon exchanging wedding vows, the balance on the card—which now includes the cost of the rings—becomes part of the normal household expenses. My wife explained to her co-worker that this had not been the case in our relationship. She may have been somewhat proud of me when she told her co-worker I had paid cash for her ring and didn't bring any bills (except a mortgage payment) to the marriage.

When Lesia and I started dating and I realized she might become the future Mrs. Riddick, I started saving money. Prior to asking her to marry me I had conducted informal interviews with many couples who had been married for years. One standard question was, "What was one of the biggest things you fought over during your early years of marriage?" The answer I kept hearing was: *MONEY!* Because of these experiences, I promised myself that money would never be a problem in my marriage.

Lesia's engagement ring cost about what you would pay for a used car in very good condition. If I could not pay for it in cash, I would have re-evaluated the size or saved longer to avoid financing a piece of jewelry.

I have been money-conscious throughout the majority of my life. There have been a few times I have been foolish but, if I had to take an average, I would say I have understood *value* most of the time. If I were to ask Lesia to describe my relationship with money in one word, she would say, "Cheap." I prefer the term *frugal* (i.e., sparing or economical with money). I can think of an instance where she mentioned to me that the TV in our bedroom was leaning slightly to the left. I fixed it Al's way. I stacked four pennies on top of each other and sat them on the left side of the cable box which balanced it perfectly. She created a FaceBook post with a picture which read, "This is how my husband fixed the leaning TV."

If you want to amuse yourself, watch how people act when they talk about themselves and money. You will notice some think they are better than others because they earn large sums of money on an annual basis or live in a huge house in an upscale neighborhood. You will also notice people who may not earn as much… but seem happier than those who do. I used to wonder why this occurred until I came to discover that money can't make you happy. I have heard this a million times, but some things you have to learn yourself through experience.

Recently I had lunch with a gentleman whose business associate is worth several hundred million dollars. Although this guy is financially secure, his extended family relationships are a mess and his immediate family is unhappy. This description could be applicable to a family with an average household income. The only difference is that one family has more stuff to fight over than the other.

The gentleman with whom I was having lunch made an interesting point regarding the financial lessons his son is learning. He said, "I told my son that if he ever finances something that depreciates in value, he's proving that he doesn't understand money and that he's an idiot." I immediately started thinking about some of the purchases I had financed over my lifetime. The only item that appreciated in value is our house. You may be thinking about the things you have financed—or continue to finance—at this very moment. Have they appreciated or depreciated in value?

Do you consider how much money you need to earn in order to have a certain amount of cash in your hand? For example, assume you have a friend who is single, lives in Ohio and wants to purchase, with cash, a used car priced at $8,925 ($9,527.44 including sales tax). In order to have $9,527.44 in cash, your friend needs to earn considerably more than this. Here's a breakdown of the extra money required to buy that car:

$602.44 Hamilton County, Ohio sales tax

$141.56 Ohio income taxes

$892.50 (10% federal tax bracket, tax on earnings up to $8,925)

$90.37 (15% tax bracket, tax on earnings above $8,925—$602.44)

$590.70 (6.2% Social Security)

$138.15 (1.45% Medicare)

$11,380.72 (actual amount that would have to be earned to pay cash)

The used car which has a list price of $8,925, costs an extra $2,455.72 because of taxes in order to gain access to $9,527.44 cash. This example may cause you to rethink the process of buying a new car, which rapidly depreciates in value.

Money is difficult to earn, costs more than you think, and is easy to spend. Now that you have read my car buying example, I am sure you understand why creating a monthly spending plan is critical. Counting your money develops your ability to comprehend its true value. Are you beginning to look at your spending habits in a different light?

Money changes people. This is true to some degree. However, if you are impolite and earn meager wages, you may remain impolite after making significantly more. I will never forget watching Deion Sanders (former Dallas Cowboys corner) being interviewed on TBN (Trinity Broadcasting Network). He said, *"Money only makes you more of what you already are."* That is an accurate statement. Individuals who are philanthropic will increase their giving after they accumulate wealth.

Never develop income envy. This occurs when you become upset because of the wages earned by someone else. Use that energy determining how to increase your income, cash flow, or skills. This can lead to a better life for you and your family. People get upset with rich people, but almost no one gets upset with someone who's broke. Interesting! Deep down, I bet people with "income envy" or "wealth envy" feel as though the person with money knows something they don't.

If there isn't anything wrong with achieving the goal of being broke, why is there something wrong with wanting to achieve the goal of being financially solvent?

Chapter 9

BUDGET: THE SIX-LETTER DIRTY WORD

Budgeting is one of the most necessary, yet most neglected, life skills of today. People who do not budget often find their daily finances in a constant state of chaos, yet they fail to take action to remedy the situation. Since I began Game Time Budgeting, a financial education firm, I have been amazed at the different emotional and oral responses I observe when mentioning the "B" word. Remember when you were 10 years old and accidentally said a curse word in front of your parents? Maybe you recall the first time your child said a four-letter word in your presence. That look of astonishment is the same way people respond to me when I talk about the *benefits of budgeting*. Living by a monthly budget has the same effect on your money as rainfall does to your lawn. *It helps your money grow.*

Where did the negative connotation attached to the word budget originate? According to worldwidewords.org:

> *The origin of our word budget is the Latin bulga, a little pouch or knapsack, which may have come from a Gaulish source that's related to the Irish bolg, "bag". The word turned up in English in the fifteenth century, having travelled via the French bougette, a diminutive form of bouge, "leather bag". Its first meaning in English indeed was "pouch, wallet, bag," and followed its French original in usually implying something made of leather.*

I can only guess that, over the years, the word budget was associated with not having much money since its first English meanings were "pouch, wallet, and bag." Only small quantities of cash can fit in these items so I am assuming that is where the negativity originated. Regardless of how unpopular budgeting is today, it is one of the most responsible things you can do specific to money.

I am constantly approached by individuals with questions regarding how they can make sense out of their dollars. Some say they want to become more efficient managers of their money; others express their desire to create a better life for themselves and their children. Facial expressions and body language change after I mention 'budgeting.' Remember this: *It is difficult to measure your success with money if you do not track it.*

Can you imagine a multi-billion dollar company in America operating without a budget? I am 99.9% positive that companies generating massive amounts of revenue did not open on their first day of business and find themselves at the billion-dollar roundtable. They accomplished this through creative revenue-generating strategies and wise budgeting techniques. Maintain attentiveness to your dollars and cents. If you respect them, they will treat you similarly. The Center for Responsive Politics analyzed 2012 personal financial disclosure records of Congress and discovered more than half had an average net worth of over one million dollars. Does this make you wish government was as scrupulous with your tax dollars as they are with their personal finances? Unfortunately, most people don't treat other people's money like their own. This book is not about politics so let us take a look at what a budget is and is not.

A budget is:

- A plan for your monthly finances that takes into account expenses and various sources of income.
- A real-world model of what you can and cannot do with your money within a certain amount of time.
- A document that can assist you in accomplishing your goals.
- An itemized list of what you plan to do with your money over a week, month, quarter, or year.
- A list of instructions for your money.
- Something that can make you happy, sad and angry all within 10 seconds.

A budget is not:

- A death sentence.
- An admission ticket to the house of pain, suffering, and frustration.

- Something that restricts you. A budget only shows you what is, and is not, financially possible.
- An excuse to throw a temper tantrum like a child even though you may be over 21 years old.
- The worst mathematical exercise of your life. (I think that might be a tie between Geometry and Calculus.)

I once completed an entire Geometry test and scored a zero. If a guy like that can grow up to become debt-free, I am sure *your* financial success potential is boundless.

Chapter 10

UNDERSTANDING YOUR MONEY EMOTIONS

P eople do most things because they can—and because it feels good. I'll never forget the day I asked Andrew, my youngest nephew (approximately age five at the time), why he ate six slices of pizza? He replied, *"Because I wanted to."* That response was genuine. He could have also said, "Because I felt like it and I did it." We make similar statements to ourselves to justify behaviors with money. *Feelings* are the results of your beliefs and thoughts which dictate action. If you have a bad day at work, buying yourself a new outfit is the action you might take to *feel* better. This is called *retail therapy*. When you are controlled solely by your emotions, you tend to eliminate logic.

Feelings then drive you toward actions you may not otherwise commit—and often later regret.

I was told a story about a man who visited a Corvette dealership to observe what he called his dream car. A salesperson introduced himself and began asking questions which revealed the man's love of Corvettes. This gentleman, to his wife's dismay, financed (rented) a new car for the sum of $600 per month. Renting occurs when you make payments on a car you do not own.

Everyone attaches emotions to money. Only a robot could avoid this. One day, Lesia and I were riding through the parking lot of a nearby pharmacy and noticed something blowing across the pavement which appeared to be money. Upon closer inspection, I found that it was. I told Lesia to stop the car so I could get out and pick up this free gift. I looked around to see if there was anyone looking for it so I could return the money. Once confirming the owner was not in the parking lot, I kept it. Did my wife and I get excited? Of course! In fact, as I am writing this I'm remembering that I placed the money in her glove compartment and it hasn't been touched since. We found $6 and you would have thought we won the lottery! Maybe we'll treat ourselves to ice cream at some point.

Recently, while climbing the steps to the main floor of our ranch-style house, my wife yelled, "I think there's a leak in the basement." After investigating the small amount of water near the base of a wall, I surmised there might be a small crack in the foundation, which is where the leak must have originated. We had recently experienced several days of continuous rain and I assumed this was the cause of the leak. *Cost* was the first thought that came to my mind. Since it is very difficult to separate emotion from money, I initially became agitated. Even though we have money set aside for emergencies, it doesn't feel good when you actually have to draw from this reserve. You can never stop experiencing emotions with money; you can only attempt to control the actions your emotions inspire.

I cut a hole in the drywall after the plumber arrived (it was too expensive for him to make the cut). I was happy to learn the upstairs toilet was leaking instead of there being a problem with the foundation. We purchased a new comfort-height toilet since we couldn't rule out the possibility that the old one contained a crack. In the past, I never paid attention to toilet seat height but, after using the comfort-height model, I like it. It's the small things in life that give me pleasure.

Lesia requested I never reveal the following story, however, I think it's a perfect example of the link between emotions and money. During 2013, we traveled to Beverly Hills, California, for our 11-year anniversary celebration. We usually travel internationally for this event, but Lesia's doctor advised against it as she was dealing with a recent medical issue. As you can imagine, everything in Beverly Hills is ridiculously expensive. We spent as much money in one week in Beverly Hills as we would have spent flying to the Caribbean and staying at an all-inclusive resort for seven days.

While dining at an Italian restaurant one evening, I could not finish my meal. This is a rare occurrence because I love to eat. I carried my leftovers to our hotel and planned on eating them the next day. The next morning I discovered, to my disappointment, there was no microwave in our room. I found this peculiar, but then began to understand it was by design. Consider this: Lesia and I were at the nicest hotel in Beverly Hills. Judging by the looks of most of the guests and the cars they were driving—Ferraris, Bentleys, Maseratis— eating leftovers likely was not a part of their daily regimen. However, for a small town guy like me, it was time to practice ingenuity. I plugged the power cord of an iron into an electrical outlet and placed the iron hot side up on top of a trash can. Because my food was packaged in an aluminum container, the makeshift stove top worked perfectly.

My breakfast pasta was one of the best meals I have tasted, especially since ordering an omelet from the hotel restaurant cost $24. You may be thinking, "This guy is cheap." I prefer the phrase, *saving connoisseur*. My secret is out. Don't judge.

*Who needs a microwave when
an iron will do?*

Chapter 11

MARRIAGE: A PARTNERSHIP WITH FINANCIAL PERKS

O ctober 23, 1999 was the day I first laid eyes on Lesia. She was a new Cincinnati resident and would now call this city home after completing her Master's Degree in Mechanical Engineering. I often tell people she is the brainpower and I am the mouthpiece. When Lesia arrived in Cincinnati, I had been living here for approximately one year. The group I hung around, at that time, shared a common bond since none of us were native Cincinnatians. On this particular night, approximately 20 of us met at Show-case Cinemas in Springdale, Ohio to watch *The Best Man*. My wife rode with our mutual friend, Marian, whom she met while completing her undergraduate studies at Tennessee State University. By the time everyone was seated inside the theatre, Lesia and I were sitting beside each other. She hasn't been able to get rid of me since.

A year and a half had passed since Lesia and I began dating. One evening we were having a phone conversation when she asked the question most men hate to hear: "Where is this relationship going?" Unbeknownst to Lesia, I had posed that question to myself numerous times. I began stating some of the qualities she possessed which I desired in a wife: spiritual, intelligent, honest, kind, empathetic, and possessing a good sense of humor. In addition, a pretty face, hands, and feet were icing on the cake. When I finished speaking, Lesia did not utter a word. I think she was in shock because I had answered her question with clarity and thoughtfulness. Lesia never posed that question again. Waiting patiently was her next challenge, knowing I would eventually pop the question.

I have been asked how I knew Lesia was the woman I was to marry. Simple…I received a sign from God. After deciding to ask for her hand in holy matrimony, I recall saying my prayers and asking God to confirm she was the one. I woke up the next morning with a feeling of peace I had never experienced. The following day I drove downtown to A. R. Jester (now Jester Jewelers on the West Side) and purchased Lesia's engagement ring. Until that point in my life, I had never spent such a large sum of money on one purchase.

Our wedding day

Because I am a *saving connoisseur*, I often make financial decisions some people would classify as abnormal. Prior to purchasing Lesia's engagement ring, I had learned paying sales tax could be avoided by shipping it out of state. Sales tax on a one-carat almost flawless diamond is expensive. I contacted my friend, Terri, who lived in Indianapolis and received permission to ship the ring to her address. The drive to Indianapolis from Cincinnati is approximately an hour and a half. Spending three hours in my car and a small amount on gas to save several hundred dollars in sales tax qualifies as a good deal in my mind.

My proposal entailed asking Lesia to marry me on the two-year anniversary of the date we met, October 23. Before driving to her apartment, I decided to purchase two long-stemmed roses which I hid outside, near the front entrance. I knocked on the door and my beautiful bride-to-be was standing there without any idea of what was about to happen. I strolled into Lesia's apartment and she asked me to ride with her to the store. After we walked out the garage door, I created an excuse to re-enter her apartment. I ran quickly to the front door, secured the two long-stemmed roses, and brought them inside. I placed them in an area where Lesia likely would look after returning from the store. She loves to cook, so I am almost certain we went to pick up a missing recipe ingredient.

She parked her car in the garage, walked through the door, and saw the roses. Excitedly she asked, "What are these for?" I replied, "They're to celebrate the two-year anniversary of the day we first met." She replied, "Aw, that's so sweet." I walked into the kitchen. My heart was pounding to the point where I could hear it. I poured a glass of milk to drink with my ginger snap cookies. I knocked the carton of milk over exposing my nervousness. Milk spilled on the counter which agitated me because I wanted the evening to be perfect. Lesia said, "Al, it's just milk. Calm down!" She was unaware the spilled milk was interfering with my game plan.

I cleaned the counter and began explaining how much I had enjoyed our relationship during the past two years. I expressed what she meant to me and that I loved having her in my life. My heartfelt sentiments caused nostalgic feelings and Lesia suggested we watch *The Best Man* (video) since it was the movie we watched after meeting two years ago. She was sitting on my lap but got up to walk toward the television so she could find the VHS tape (Keep in mind, the year was 2001). I said, with her back facing me, "I've been telling you these things because there's something I want to ask you." Lesia turned to look at me. I was down on one knee with a white ring box in my hand. She ran towards me as though she had been launched from a rocket, extended her ring finger and I said, "It would be an honor to have you as my wife. Will you marry me?"

Lesia was shaking uncontrollably. I held her hand steady while placing the ring on her finger. Immediately, Lesia began sprinting around her apartment jumping, yelling, and screaming for joy. Although I had asked for her hand in marriage, she had not answered my question. Time stood still while I was down on one knee observing Lesia's excitement. She noticed me (after what seemed to be 15 minutes) and said, "Yes! I would love to be your wife." A few months later, Lesia informed me she slept, that night, with her hand purposely positioned so the engagement ring would be seen first after opening her eyes the next morning.

Money disputes is one of the main reasons marriages end in divorce. To circumvent this obstacle, Lesia and I often discussed how money would be handled after we became man and wife. Prior to beginning this new chapter in our lives, each of us could be 100% selfish. When you are single, it takes only one vote to have a majority rule. Once married, too much selfishness can become a barrier to marital success. Selfishness is a forerunner to money problems. There is no such thing as a perfect marriage; however, marriage can become exponentially more difficult when couples refuse to work together as a team.

The advantages of marriage far outweigh the disadvantages. If both spouses work, there is an obvious financial benefit (usually). When you are single, you become accustomed to earning 100% of the household income and paying 100% of the expenses. I am sure someone reading this might say, *I'd rather have it that way than spend the rest of my life with someone who gets on my nerves.* Keep in mind that you likely get on his or her nerves, too. It's fun partnering together in managing household finances. *It can also propel you toward hitting your goals at a faster pace.*

After Lesia and I were married, we opened a joint bank account. Our paychecks were deposited into this account from which all our bills were paid. We agreed to pay ourselves an allowance from the joint account, as well. Some people laugh when they hear Lesia and I have an allowance. Call it what you wish…a monthly stipend or fun money…but it is a specific amount of money we each get to spend every month, no questions asked. These funds are transferred automatically from our joint account to each of our personal accounts by the first or second day of each month. Our agreement dictates the other spouse can't say anything about how the money is spent. It is one of the smartest financial decisions we made after exchanging our vows. By the time this book is published, we will have celebrated thirteen years of marriage and this system is still in place. When something works, why change it?

When each spouse has their own agreed upon monthly allowance, this overshadows the need to sneak around trying to hide purchases you don't want your spouse to know about. I love when my wife goes shopping, comes home and models her new clothes for me. It's difficult to become upset about that.

One of the first things you notice after getting married and combining household incomes is the size of your joint account. Some couples tend to lose their sense of discipline when discovering this perceived pot of gold at the end of their rainbow. If they are not careful, to their astonishment, they may wake up a few years later and discover they are broke. As a word of caution, I would not combine money with that special someone until *after* the wedding. However, it is acceptable if both parties are contributing a specific amount of money from each paycheck to fund the wedding. It would be a frightening experience to discover the person with whom you were to say 'I do' has had a change of heart and now says 'I don't.'

After Lesia and I married, the amount I was accustomed to seeing deposited on payday doubled. She could say the same thing. This is the first advantage of getting married—your household income increases. This can have a *negative* or *positive* impact. For us, we had agreed already on how the money in this account would be utilized. One of the rules we live by is: ***Become broke on purpose, not by accident.*** We believe in instructing every dollar that flows through our household to have purpose, direction, and an assignment. *If you don't tell money what to do and how to act, it will misbehave.* To reach our monthly goal of becoming *broke on purpose*, we allocate the net income flowing through our household so that income minus expenses equals zero. I am reminded of the Staples commercial with the button that reads: *That was easy.*

The second financial advantage to getting married is that *eliminating debt* is the responsibility of the couple, not the individual. Think about a team sport or activity you have been involved in at some point during your lifetime. Can you imagine playing against a team by yourself? You will lose *every* time and that is not fun. When you get married, your mindset should—has to—shift if you want your marriage to last. When Lesia and I became Mr. and Mrs. Riddick, I did not have either student loan debt or auto loan debt… but she did. During our money discussions, I inserted statements such as, "*We* need to pay off *our* student loan" or "*We* should think about paying off *our* auto loan." If I had come into our marriage with a purely selfish frame of mind, one where I thought: *Those are your loans, Lesia, so you need to pay them off*, I believe that would have created a significant division within our household. Also, she may have felt as though she was married in name only.

Let's recap the first two advantages of getting married: *Number 1*—Your household income increases; *Number 2*—Individual debt becomes household debt. The *third* advantage of getting married is—*your total household expenses should decrease*. If your household *income increases* and individual *expenses decrease* because one of you has now moved in with the other, you should see a *positive financial difference* in your lives. Most newly married couples make the mistake of increasing their standard of living because they assume there is more money at their disposal. This is true and it is also not true. It *is true* because there *is* more money coming into the household. It is *not true* because (if you're managing the money correctly) the additional funds you *think you have* need to be going toward establishing a rainy-day fund, savings, paying down debt, or investing for retirement.

Too often when couples become married it seems similar to winning the lottery. Upon conquering *Powerball* or *Mega Millions*, the unexpected increase in wealth causes the winner to become more of who they were prior to cashing their winning ticket. Individuals exhibiting recklessness with their finances before getting married (i.e., hitting the mini-lottery) are prone to exhibit the same behaviors during marriage unless they receive the proper counseling or coaching. People mistakenly believe winning the lottery will solve their financial problems. If they have *low financial IQ* the day before their winning numbers are selected, they *will not* become financially smarter because they now have more money.

I calculated, recently, that my wife and I live on 54% of our take-home pay. We have the freedom to do whatever we want with 46% of our monthly net income. I don't know your household income. Whatever the number might be, if 46% of it were remaining after all mandatory expenses were paid, what type of difference might that make in your life?

The *fourth* and final financial advantage of getting married is the opportunity to *exponentially increase annual net worth. Developing a financial system with your spouse, living below your means, following the plan for saving, paying down debt, and investing should produce measurable growth in net worth.* Since 2002, Lesia and I have tracked yearly changes in our net worth. I shared the following story with readers of the *Game Time Budgeting Newsletter* in August of 2013:

*On July 27, 2013 at 7:56 p.m., after updating our net worth tracking spreadsheet, I discovered that my wife and I had realized one of our long-term goals—**a minimum net worth of $1,000,000**. It's hard to describe the emotions I felt when I noticed there were seven digits to the left of the decimal point. I was excited, motivated, energized, and* *encouraged, just to name a few. Here's the background to our story:*

*We were married in August of 2002. At that time, our year-end net worth (assets minus liabilities) was **$82,401**. We weren't as disciplined with money then as we are now, so we hadn't saved as aggressively as we could have. After learning to respect every dollar of income generated, we made a commitment to give our money better purpose and direction. We increased our pre-tax and after-tax savings and decided to eliminate our debt, as well. Listed below are a few highlights from our journey:*

- ***1,121%—Net worth increase over 11 years → $1,000,000***
- *$152,711—Largest increase in net worth over a one-year span.*
- *($19,217)—Largest decrease in net worth over a one-year span.*
- *2007—Year we successfully eliminated all debt.*
- *2010—Year I was laid off from my $100,000+ per year job, which slashed our household income in* half. *(I went full time at Game Time Budgeting the next day.)*
- *Automobiles—My wife drives a 13-year-old car and I drive a 5-year-old car.*

- *Charitable donations—Current largest monthly household expense.*
- *16%—Current amount of gross income saved each month.*

Points of interest:

- *My wife and I usually eat out at restaurants where we have a coupon.*
- *We take vacations only if there's enough money available to pay for them in cash.*
- *We're still somewhat spontaneous with money, but we realize there's a consequence for every financial decision we make.*

Maximize your financial potential. If you aspire to save more, spend with wisdom, and increase your net worth, you can do it if you create a plan, practice discipline, adjust your financial behaviors, and *NEVER QUIT*. Money follows the instructions you give it. Lesia and I told our money to help us create a million-dollar net worth before age 40 and it complied with our orders. We achieved this goal at age 38.

I purposely omitted discussing income because it is not as important as you may think. The main point is my wife and I committed to a plan and achieved the desired result. Accomplishing the goal required 11 years of commitment and focused intensity.

I do not consider us wealthy because we wake up each morning and have to work for income. Wealthy people choose whether to work, or not. However, I think we possess a millionaire mindset which was developed years ago. Ironically, more than a decade elapsed before our actual net worth caught up to the vision we always knew existed for us.

I conducted an Internet search and discovered there are approximately 10.1 million households in the United States with $1 million or more in investable assets, excluding the value of their primary residence (Source: Spectrem Group, a Chicago-based research firm). Another book I read recently, *The Wealth Choice*, by Dennis Kimbro, stated there were approximately 35,000 African-American millionaires in the United States at the end of 2009. To know my wife and I are now in this category is somewhat mind-boggling. I wonder how many African-American couples under age 40 in the United States have a million-dollar net worth?

According to Spectrem Group, the average U.S. millionaire is 62 years old and only 1% of millionaires are under age 35. Despite your perceptions about millionaires, my wife and I do not live an extravagant lifestyle. If we attended a millionaire's convention, I am positive we would be the couple asked to leave after being accused of impersonating millionaires.

Chapter 12

LEARN FROM YOUR MISTAKES

While cleaning my dresser on a sunny Sunday morning, I discovered a real estate tax bill displaying a 30-day old due date. Panic immediately seized my body as I thought, *Oh, my God! Did I pay this bill?* Shock and disbelief were the emotions I experienced next because the bill had not been filed away. Paying the amount due and placing the document in the year-end tax deduction folder was my normal custom. Furthermore, I had not written the word "PAID" on the real estate tax bill as done numerous times in the past. My heart rate increased as I began to speculate about the late fee on this four-figure past due debt. Paying a late fee is the cost incurred for being careless and irresponsible.

Every action in the Riddick household stopped immediately while I investigated the situation. First, I entered our log-in information to check the online account from which we routinely withdraw funds to pay real estate taxes. Frustration set in after I did not locate a withdrawal matching the amount on the bill. Next, I searched an alternate account and did not find the corresponding withdrawal amount there either. Now exasperated, I could not fathom that I had neglected to pay a bill. I checked one final account as my last resort. My feelings of frustration, confusion, and disbelief subsided after discovering I had paid the bill one month before its due date.

I shared this story with Lesia, somewhat reluctantly. She laughed and said, "I bet your heart stopped when you thought that bill was late." I replied, "You know it almost did. What kind of a man would I be if I talk about the importance of fiscal responsibility and then pay a bill late?" During a recent conversation with my wife, she said, "You're a man of integrity and that's why I respect you." When I thought I was past due on a bill, I felt as if I was not living up to my expectations or those of my wife.

That incident reminded me of the following lessons:

1. **Create and follow a financial process**. I write "PAID" (usually) on the real estate tax bill and place it in the appropriate file. However, on this occasion, I paid the bill while using a computer downstairs, transported it upstairs to our bedroom, and placed it on my dresser. Financial confusion is created by not having a system in place for managing money and paying bills.

2. **Financial disorganization wastes time and energy.** I invested approximately five minutes solving the payment status of the real estate tax bill. I became angry at myself—not to mention disappointed—for no reason. Had I followed my normal routine (i.e., the system), I would not have been sidetracked with such foolishness.

How would you describe your financial process for saving, paying bills, spending, and investing? Stay the course if you are happy with your results. If not, implement new processes and systems today.

Beware of Cyberthieves!

On September 29, 2013, I received an e-mail from what appeared to be my bank stating the following:

> *For security reasons, access to your online banking has been disabled due to a* ***recent security upgrade****. In order to regain access, follow the reference below to an instant verification process.*

My brain was switched to "off" while I was attempting to multitask and I clicked the link. Immediately, I said, "That was stupid." I called my bank to tell them about the suspicious e-mail. They informed me that cyber-criminals sometimes send out phishing (also called carding or spoofing) e-mails in an effort to gain electronic access to banking accounts to steal money. These e-mails are filled with malware (a conjunction of **mali**cious soft**ware**), any kind of unwanted programming that is installed without your consent.

After conversing with a branch manager, I logged into our bank's website to ensure no money was stolen from our accounts. Upon inspection, all balances appeared to be correct. Not more than one minute later, I received an e-mail informing me a new payee had been created from one of our accounts. I dialed the customer service call center for our banking institution. The representative instructed me to contact their fraud protection unit the next morning because business hours had ended for the day.

Lesia and I continued our discussion regarding the new payee email. I placed a second call to customer service to ask additional questions. We were dumbfounded when informed a cybercriminal had created a future payment (due in one week) from our account. Our bank would have cut the check had we not cancelled it. The representative explained the process of how our money would have been returned after filing a claim. If the check had not been cancelled, we were still responsible for covering payments to various service providers until the situation was resolved. If our account had insufficient funds after receiving an electronic bill payment request, late fees may have applied. Thankfully our situation never escalated to the point where our bank applied overdraft fees due to money being stolen from our account.

The next morning, I called fraud protection. Lesia and I were startled when the inspector informed us the malware program had attempted to issue a second check. It failed. The customer service representative from the previous day's conversation blocked online access. Our username and password had been updated as well. Jokingly, I said to Lesia, "If I were a criminal, I wouldn't have waited a week to issue myself a check. I would have created a command that cut the check on the same day I hacked someone's account." I guess our *cyber thief* thought about this, as well, and decided to issue a more timely payment with the second attempt.

This incident prompted me to research cybercrime. *The 2013 Identity Fraud Report,* released in February 2013 by Javelin Strategy & Research, reports that in 2012 identity fraud incidents increased by more than one million victims and fraudsters stole more than $21 billion…the highest amount since 2009. Based on rough estimates, that is equivalent to stealing approximately $70 from every citizen in the U.S. Contrary to popular opinion, the saying "crime doesn't pay" is not 100% accurate. It pays until you get caught.

My knowledge regarding *cyber theft* increased because of this ordeal. The *malware* was designed to create a payment. The *cyber thief* was able to access our account because my keystrokes were captured automatically when I checked the online balances. We modified each of our accounts and corresponding login information. I called the major credit reporting agencies (TransUnion, Experian, Equifax) and initiated a fraud alert in case my personal information became compromised. I ordered a new debit card after learning my card number was electronically linked to the username on my bank's website. Check your card to determine if yours is linked. I also had my computer swept (i.e., cleaned) to remove all potential threats.

Always use caution before clicking on links. Here are a few items to ask yourself and consider:

- What personal information are you sharing on various forms of social media that could be used to compromise your identity?
- Have you considered how mobile phones and tablets often use non-secure wireless networks and third-party apps to make it easier to access your personal information?

- Protect your wireless network with a password.
- Disable the auto-login feature on your apps. What if your phone or tablet is stolen?
- Download and update mobile anti-virus software.

It is nearly impossible to locate a cybercriminal. The malware they employ uses different IP addresses to avoid being tracked. My failed attempt to multitask almost cost Lesia and I $3,000. The bill for having my computer swept was $75. That is a small price to pay compared to the sum the *cyber thief* tried to steal. If I had been more attentive, the entire situation could have been avoided for $0.

Everyone, at some point, encounters a financial challenge or commits an unintelligent act with money. If the lesson you learn is not too costly, consider it one experience on your financial journey.

Chapter 13

ATTITUDE IMPACTS OUTCOME

Attitude, according to Google, is a settled way of thinking or feeling about someone or something, typically one that is reflected in a person's behavior.

Most adults can name at least one individual who became successful despite the environment in which they were raised, lack of education, or economic opportunity. I love reading books that chronicle someone's journey to success. The story details are often better than the end result. For example, my wife is a Michael Jackson fan. After his death, I remember watching a television program that detailed his life growing up in Gary, Indiana. It told of the countless hours he invested honing his craft while practicing songs and dance moves with his brothers. Although Michael Jackson's dad may have planted the seed for his son's career in the entertainment industry, at some point, Michael developed a *can-do* attitude, which propelled him toward superstar status.

One of the best personal examples I recall of attitude impacting outcome occurred during my sophomore year in college. My dad and I made a bet based on my ability to earn a 4.0 GPA for a semester. If I won, he had to purchase a new car stereo for my Chevrolet Beretta. Fancy stereo systems and loud speakers were trendy at the time. I remember thinking, *I may not have ever made all 'As' in the past, but now, since a new car stereo is on the line, I know I can do it.* I do not remember what I wagered if I had lost. I studied more the following semester than at any point in my life. When I received my grades, I had earned all *'As.'* I retained my new study habits after learning what more effort could accomplish. The bar had now been raised. It is amazing what someone can do when they are motivated.

Each time I looked at the new stereo, after its installation, I remembered having set a goal and putting forth the effort to achieve it.

I have always believed I could do whatever I set my mind to since I was a little boy. If I asked my parents and sister why I am this way, they might say, "He's just too stubborn to fail." I have been accused of being hard-headed a time or two—or a dozen, according to my wife. Failure is not an option when I focus my mind on a goal I want to achieve. I recall seeing a social media post which read: *"Remember that failure is an event not a person."* (Zig Ziglar) When challenged, I develop an intense desire that refuses to give up or give in until the goal is achieved. This trait has positive and negative attributes. My actions have been insane (not because of a chemical imbalance) a few times in my life. I can become so consumed with performing a task one way— my way–that I am blinded to faster and more efficient ways to produce the desired result. Becoming an entrepreneur has helped me overcome this barrier to success.

Your money attitude can impact your financial outcome. Earlier I mentioned that attitude is a settled way of thinking or feeling about something—in this case, money.

Here are a few examples of various attitudes people may exhibit about money:

1. I was born broke and I am going to die broke.
2. My parents did not leave me an inheritance so how can I achieve financial success?
3. I think wealthy people are crooks.
4. Why should I think I can save money when I have not been able to do it so far?
5. If only I had more financial discipline.
6. I was born broke but I refuse to die broke.
7. I do not need an inheritance from my parents; I can make my own money.
8. I should study the behaviors of wealthy people if I ever want to become wealthy.
9. If other people can learn how to save money, I can, too.
10. Discipline, with money, is a behavior that can be learned.

I read an interesting quote by Henry Ford, founder of Ford Motor Company: *"Whether you think you can, or you think you can't—you're right."* I have proved this statement to myself on multiple occasions.

Recall the last time you overcame a challenging situation. It may not have involved money. Maybe it concerned initiating an exercise regimen, ending a relationship, or facing a fear of public speaking. Success is discovered by moving forward, one block north after crossing Fear Street.

During my late teens, I would often shy away from situations that required me facing my fears. I was most afraid of speaking in public. To overcome this fear, I purposely placed myself in situations where I had to break down my perceived barrier to success. Today, I can speak in a room with hundreds of people, in front of a television camera, or in a radio studio without getting an upset stomach. The butterflies in my stomach have not gone away. Now I experience them because of passion and excitement, not because I am afraid.

During my time as an entrepreneur, it has become evident how attitude impacts outcome. When I first started **Game Time Budgeting**, I underestimated the value of the services and coaching I was providing. My focus was getting _hired_ which would provide an opportunity to help people improve their financial lives. When calculating the preparation time, travel time, and speaking time, in actuality, I was paying people to hire me (not a good long-term business strategy). It did not take long to discover the error of my ways and adjust my fee scale accordingly.

Your attitude and behaviors toward personal finance may be a reflection of how much you think you are worth.

A few years ago, an associate expressed how difficult it would be for **Game Time Budgeting** to do business with a specific company. I thought, *Just because it was difficult for you, doesn't mean it will be difficult for me.* I could have heeded this individual's advice and quit before starting. When you do not try, failure is *guaranteed.* Not long afterward, I received a call letting me know **Game Time Budgeting** was being included in this particular company's annual budget.

Chapter 14

BECOME YOUR OWN
UNCOMMON MILLIONAIRE

My deepest desire is that this book somehow inspires you to assess your relationship with money and will help you find the success you seek. It has been a therapeutic experience explaining how my wife and I created a seven-figure net worth. Our story does not include stock tips, investments with unusually high returns, or the creation of a multi-million dollar business idea. We controlled our behaviors, eliminated debt, and saved aggressively. This is a simple formula for anyone to follow. *Unfortunately, not everyone will.* Our expedition lasted eleven years; your journey may not take quite as long. It might also take more time… depending on your specific financial situation and level of intensity. I look forward to the day when I meet people who tell me reading this book was the catalyst that prompted a financial rebirth in their lives.

When I began this writing process, I was intimidated by the idea that people might consider me arrogant for writing a book highlighting how my wife and I became millionaires before the age of 40. Realistically speaking, this book is not about Lesia and me...it *IS* about developing the habit of saving money and practicing fiscal discipline. Achieving millionaire status is the byproduct of those behaviors. I do not proclaim to be a financial wizard. However, I am confident living well below your means produces better financial results than living within or above your means. The one characteristic I possess which may set me apart from others is my ability to *practice financial discipline* instead of wishing I could.

I wonder what *legacy* the end of my financial journey will have created...if any? Actually, I am more excited about the behavioral modifications *you* will make in *your* life to achieve *your* dreams and aspirations. Through my years of speaking and facilitating financial workshops, my goal is to do what I do now until the day I die. I love it! Helping others reach their goals crystallizes my ultimate life goal.

Here is my blueprint for becoming your own uncommon millionaire.

1. **Protect your wealth-building ability.** Insurance is one of the ways in which individuals shift risks. Ensure you have the appropriate amount of life, homeowner's, renter's, and auto insurance. If your household has a net worth that exceeds the liability coverage for your homeowner's or auto insurance policies, consider a personal umbrella liability policy to protect your assets. Make sure your last will and testament is updated. If you have dependent children, document the name of the couple (or person) to whom you wish to entrust their care. Fiscal responsibility may be one of the selection criteria. Create a living will and a durable healthcare power of attorney to act on your behalf in the event you are not able to make medical decisions.

2. **Understand where your money is going.** Access your online bank statements and categorize your spending for the previous two months (e.g.,

rent/mortgage, car payment, eating out, recreation, gas, utilities, groceries, etc.). This will help uncover opportunities to decrease spending. The truth is you can only have more cash at your disposal by earning more or spending less.

3. **Decide where you want to be in the next six months or one year.** Goal setting is a practice many people avoid. Imagine a person shooting a gun without aiming. Hitting the target is impossible. When you do not set a goal, you will not know when you have arrived at your destination. If you know where you want to be, start there and work backward. The point is developing a behavior that produces your intended outcome. Lesia and I had to determine what we were willing to sacrifice in order to maximize our financial potential. You can rarely achieve any level of success, personal or professional, without some level of sacrifice.

4. **Create and follow a spending plan.** Every month, Lesia and I become broke *on purpose*. We give every dollar flowing through our household an assignment and it behaves accordingly. I use the term spending plan to avoid that six-letter dirty

word, budget. Be sure to never spend more than 30% of your monthly net income on housing (mortgage or rent), no more than 15% on transportation, and no more than 10% on debt.

5. **Create an emergency fund, a rainy day fund, or an uh-oh fund.** Do not read these words without accompanying them with action. Think about the consequences of not having an emergency fund. None of them are good. Saving $1,000 to $3,000 is an initial start. Becoming a habitual saver will allow you to accumulate at least six months of living expenses. This will not happen quickly. It may take up to two years. Money saved in your emergency fund is for a future unplanned event (e.g., unexpected job loss, major auto repairs). Regular savings is for a future planned event (e.g., vacation, birthday gift). Never get the two confused.

6. **Eliminate debt.** Credit card debt is a common theme in the lives of many people. It is one of the most expensive debts you can buy. Pay off your credit cards from smallest to highest balance. If you use credit cards to earn reward points, your focus may not be on creating wealth. Auto and student

loan debt can be paid off in the same manner as your credit cards. I suggest focusing on eliminating one debt at a time while paying the minimum amount due on others.

7. **Save for retirement**. Saving toward retirement should be a top priority. The option to pay off debt while saving for retirement is your decision. Saving at least 15% of your gross income each year should help you accumulate a respectable nest egg. The earlier you start saving, the easier it becomes.

8. **Educate yourself about personal finance.** Learning more about money has given me a different mindset and financial perspective. I do not become excited every time I read a book or magazine about a financial topic. I am a seeker of financial knowledge so I invest the time required to become less ignorant. If you do not like reading, watch videos on the Internet, stream or download Podcasts. If that does not interest you, borrow FREE audio books from your local library.

9. **Shift your money mindset.** Accomplishing any goal is difficult without first renewing your mind.

I constantly tell myself what is possible so I can maintain the proper attitude (i.e., mindset). It is easy to become complacent and inactive. This is the danger zone. To avoid this destination, I dare you to speak out loud every morning for the next three weeks what you want out of your life. Additionally, tell yourself what you like about you. Make a list of things you do well. I am trying intentionally to get you focused on your *potential*.

10. **Push through setbacks.** Like you, everything in my life has not happened the way I wished. Do not let a temporary roadblock on your road to success cause paralysis. Roadblocks can cause fear to creep into your mind. The fear you perceive in your mind is always greater than the action required to overcome it.

11. **Associate with people whom you wish to emulate.** You will never learn how to become successful financially if you spend the majority of your time around people with money problems.

10 Money Tips You May Want To Remember

1. Never take financial advice from a person who is financially broke. (That is, unless you want to learn how they became broke so you can avoid their mistakes.)

2. Money does exactly what you tell it to do.

3. Never pay retail price for any big-ticket item (i.e., anything that costs more than $500). Almost everything can be negotiated.

4. Your result is the truth. Your emotions may try to make you believe different, however, numbers usually tell the true story.

5. Do not compare your financial life to anyone else's. What you see from the outside can be very deceiving.

6. There is no such thing as good debt. The price of borrowing is always attached to an interest rate. Do you prefer to earn interest or pay interest?

7. Make the gap between income and spending as wide as possible. More cash at your disposal increases the options you have with your money.

8. You have 100% control over your savings rate.

9. Life usually gets more expensive the longer you live. Save and spend wisely.

10. Money is neither good nor bad. It is often a reflection of the person controlling it.

I appreciate your time investment to read this book. I hope you have gained a positive and helpful perspective that can be applied in your respective financial journey… or that of someone else. The principles discussed have worked in my life and I am confident they can work in yours. Let me be the first to *Congratulate you* on your current and future financial focus toward success!

END OF YEAR FINANCIAL STATUS

2002 End of Year Financial Status	2013 End of Year Financial Status
Assets	**Assets**
House—$165,000	House—$175,000
Retirement Accounts—$53,373	Retirement Accounts—$677,289
Non-retirement Accounts—$6,800	Non-retirement Accounts—$145,923
	Automobiles—$14,000
Total Assets—$225,173	**Total Assets—$1,012,212**
Liabilities	**Liabilities**
Mortgage—$120,272	Mortgage, student, & auto loans—$0
Student Loans—$5,500	
Auto Loan—$17,000	
Total Liabilities—$142,772	**Total Liabilities—$0**
NET WORTH—$82,401	**NET WORTH—$1,012,212**

Income in the previous table was purposely excluded (2013 was approximately $16,000 less than 2002). Remember, your personal savings rate is more important than how much you earn.

ABOUT THE AUTHOR

Al Riddick is President of **Game Time Budgeting** (GTB), a Cincinnati-based financial education firm. By the age of 33, Al and his wife (Lesia) achieved their *'debt-freedom'* goal. They have no mortgage, no school loans, no auto loans, and no credit card debt. Established in 2010, GTB helps individuals develop the proper mindset for spending less so they can have more. As a coach, speaker, guest columnist, and author, Al shares his passion for ***debt-free living*** by addressing the physical and emotional aspects of how people relate to money. Some of GTB's clients include Procter & Gamble, Toyota, Macy's, UPS, and Kroger. Game Time Budgeting was honored in 2015 as a *Cincinnati Children's Museum Difference Maker*.

ALSO BY AL RIDDICK

The Financial Fitness Playbook
A step-by-step guide to unleashing
tomorrow's possibilities
(Free software included)

This workbook provides practical advice and interactive worksheets to assist on your journey to **financial fitness**. Each of the 14 lessons and training exercises will equip you with the proper money mindset, information, and tools to create a more favorable financial future.

Money $mart Teens

*48 interactive lessons for understanding,
making, saving, and spending money*

Challenge, Educate, and **Equip** today's youth to enhance their financial fitness. This workbook makes learning about money fun and exciting through a variety of exercises that are:

- Engaging
- Educational
- Entertaining
- Thought-provoking
- Real world financial scenarios

**Facilitator guide available for teaching
in a group setting**

Get quantity discounts on orders of 25 or more copies.

www.GameTimeBudgeting.com